1996

Antwerp   Museum of Contemporary Art Antwerp (MUHKA)

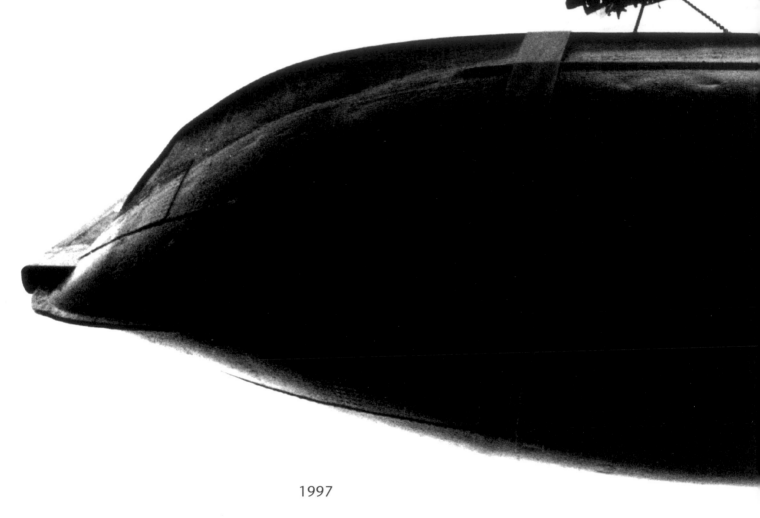

1997

Duisburg   Lehmbruck Museum of modern sculpture

Düsseldorf   City harbour

Hanover   Sprengel Museum of modern art

Max Couper
The Plot

Published 1998 by
Booth-Clibborn Editions
12 Percy Street
London W1P 9FB

Published in association with
The University of Antwerp (RUCA) 'Art on the Campus'
Groenenborgerlaan 171, 2020 Antwerp, Belgium
in collaboration with Professor Emeritus Emile Vanlommel

On the occasion of an exhibition of photographs from the book
at The European Parliament, Brussels
and the London Borough of Wandsworth
Pump House Gallery, Battersea Park

Book concept: Max Couper
Co-editor: Luise Seppeler
Design consultant: Peter Wilder
Photographic consultant: Mark Howard
Copy editor: Katharine Jacobson
Reproduction: Colour Bytes

Photography: Max Couper, Edward Woodman,
                         Michael Wiegandt, Luise
                         Seppeler, Bernd Nanninga,
                         Michael Herling

With assistance and special thanks for the book to
Professor Dr Willy Winkelmans, Professor Dr Walter Decleir,
Josiane Winkelmans, Veerle Emboo, Nick Skeens, Muriel Rees,
and Alain Bernard of Dredging International

ISBN 1-86154-123-6

info@internos.co.uk
www.booth-clibborn-editions.co.uk

Printed in Belgium

Max Couper, 2nd from right, with Luise Seppeler and Sprengel Museum crane operators

Max Couper in his time

Marina Vaizey

Max Couper: water, petroleum, steel, and mud; four countries, three museums, and four cities. A series called *The Plot* unfolded over time from the Thames in London where it was plotted, across the waterways of northern Europe over eighteen months, involving the artist and waterman Max Couper, his maps, his charts, his tug Pablo, and a barge.

Incorporated in the on-going work were notions not only of travel but also of differing roads of activity, of traditional modes of travel subverted and changed by the self consciousness of the artist. Traditional skills were needed, of navigation, of the knowledge of how to sail, of chart reading, of the permissions needed to move from country to country. The tug itself came from time to time to rest on dry land, winched and craned, to leave its imprint. This book is about the souvenirs of those events, for all that remains of a work executed through time and travel is its record, part document, part documentary, part artwork.

Couper's art draws attention not only to time – and work, work literally in keeping afloat – but to the interplay between nature and artifice, the man made and the natural. The boats are steel; they are powered by petroleum, fossil fuel, extracted and refined, the black gold of the industrial age, the fuel of heating, electricity, transport, and travel. The rivers and the waterways have been teased, altered, by human intervention, but they also have a life of their own, support lives other than human. And the efficacy of transport, with its network of permissions by human hands – the bureaucracy of northern Europe – and the skill of the human navigator, the sailor, is also at the mercy of natural happenings, of currents and tides, of weather.

This is a book of works in progress over a period of time – of installations, performances, and the souvenirs, reminiscences, remainders, and reminders of times past. In these works the footprints and imprints of forms, and the moulds and casings are of as much import as that which they contained. The frame and the setting are crucial. All are part of the spectrum of visual arts as they are practiced at the end of the 20th century. It's not just what you do, but the way that you do it – and where.

It is not necessarily a new phenomenon: visual artists have long been proponents of show business, delvers in real as well as imagined time, devisors and entrepreneurs of spectacles and theatre, street performances and events. Such notable multi media figures as Inigo Jones and Peter Paul Rubens were renowned in their day for their skills in these areas.

London   Antwerp Rotterdam Duisburg Düsseldorf   Hanover

In the case of Max Couper, sculptor and event maker, his work is modified, transformed, and irradiated by the process of his daily life. He lives on and works from a series of studio barges on the Thames, moored facing east and west, a trio insinuating itself sideways into the river. It is not everybody's work place and living place that rises and falls with the tide.

Couper's art and sculpture thus revolve around boats. Boats obviously involve water and imply the notion not only of movement and transport but also of working. And the act of working is itself perhaps a metaphor: a boat sits on the surface but depends for its success on a sure knowledge of what goes on underneath, in the substance on which it rests, on which it travels. Knowing the tides, currents, and depths, is but a small part of the continual human interaction with the artifact – the boat – which, skimming the surface, is dependent for its survival on the interaction of its craftsmanship and the guidance by its human inhabitants.

Max Couper works both on his own, and with collaborators. Rather like his own tug carried on a freighter down the river, his interests and activities are individual yet not detached from the wider stream of contemporary art activity.

A recent book which charts installation art of the past thirty years, *Blurring the Boundaries*, defines installation art as site specific and multi-media. But installation art can be portable as well. Do we think of Richard Long's sculptures – arrangements of stone, or flint, or slate, shown in art galleries – as specific to the site, or as portable art work? Another strand in late 20th century art is kinetic art. The American Alexander Calder's artwork, which consists of mobile abstract forms cascading through the air, requires a flexible amount of time to appreciate the random and inventive permutations.

Earthworks and Beyond is a title that has been used to suggest artistic interference in the natural landscape. Sometimes this is just a mark of someone passing, as with Richard Long and his walks through different landscapes. Artists in the 1970s grafted their art onto the landscape. Robert Smithson's *Spiral Jetty* (1970), which has now vanished because of erosion over time, was just that – a spiral jetty curving into the Great Salt Lake, Utah. The American James Turrell is, under the aegis of his own *Skystone Foundation*, remodelling an extinct volcano in Arizona.

Theatrical traditions have often been invoked in recent art. In the post war period there have been several now classic manifestations of performance art, deliberately temporary, ephemeral. This rich area of staged art has deployed accident and spontaneity as well as control and discipline. Jean Tinguely's *Homage to New York* (1960), a piano set on fire, auto-destructed in the garden of the Museum of Modern Art; Robert Rauschenberg's orchestrated happenings and his work with the composer John Cage and choreographer Merce Cunningham exist now only in the photograph, whilst Yves Klein was on occasion the master of the illusionistic photograph; the artist in a death defying flying leap.

The ritualizing of personal experience is a formative influence on art in a way that may be characterized as post-modern. Perhaps it began with the intimacy of the impressionists. All over Europe painters turned away from the grand subjects of myth, history, and religion, to the scene of suburb and city. Taken to an extreme of concentrated intensity, the contemporary artists Gilbert & George explicitly declare their art is their life and their life is their art.

Sometimes the medium is the message but more often the message, whatever it may be, is free to use whatever medium is most appropriate.

What is fascinating about Max Couper's series of integrated events and making of objects is his intuitive exploitation of various strands of art-making today.

The Plot incorporated mini conferences and committees. In Antwerp a major performance with actors took place lit by spotlights on the rudder of the tug Pablo and televised. Charts and maps, created by the imagination of the artist, were shown in gallery and museum situations. The boats were swung out of the water onto dry land. Industrial methods and the notion of commercial construction have also been evoked. The barge was installed on a fulcrum. Pablo left an imprint in a pile of clay and sand on city ground in the museum. This imprint eventually eroded and decayed naturally.

Couper's fascination with 'black gold' – and oil after all has been a political football during almost the entire post-war period – is part of the ordinary day-to-day process. His tangles and discussions with bureaucracy also became part of the process of the series of time based events. *The Plot* incorporates travel across boundaries but, as Max Couper points out, when on the water the signs of national jurisdiction may sometimes be well nigh invisible.

So the voyage of *The Plot* has been marked by different events involving time – the vocabulary, syntax, and grammar of the ephemeral performance. *The Plot* has also been framed by the convention of the art exhibition and by the methods of installation and site specific art.

Over a substantial period, from gestation to fruition, *The Plot* has subsumed a variety of methods of making art, all integrated within this particular voyage. Time, performance, installation, the involvement of a particular site, and the placing of the discrete art object, have all had their place, as has the blurring of the boundaries between the artist's life and the artist's art. In some senses the artist here has been both chief executive and chairman of a wide variety of activities, as well as the protagonist, in collaboration with existing physical objects. Those objects, through the activity of the artist, are seen in different ways and in different contexts thoughout the course of journeys that are both literal and metaphorical. Max Couper is an individual, idiosyncratic visual voice within the wide spectrum of multi-media art.

The tug with the barge in tow, the Channel

The Plot

three museums and four cities

In the summer of 1996 Max Couper and his crew
left London in his Thames tugboat, barge in tow, to
cross the Channel.

Arriving in Antwerp, Belgium, in September, the
tugboat was lifted out of the water for a performance
to coincide with a major exhibition of Couper's
work from London in the city's Museum of
Contemporary Art.

After leaving Antwerp the tug pushed the barge to
Rotterdam, Holland, where it was loaded into a huge
ore-barge for the journey up the Rhine to the city of
Duisburg in Germany. Here, in spring 1997, the
famous Lehmbruck Museum of sculpture hosted an
exhibition of Couper's work. At the same time an
exhibition of his charts was shown in a nearby
Düsseldorf gallery on the Rhine.

In July 1997, in the city of Düsseldorf, Couper
made the public installation of *The Steel Fulcrum*
with the barge. He then continued on by canal to
Hanover where, in the same month, the final
artwork of the series, *Tug Print*, was made for the
Sprengel Museum of modern art.

Eighteen months later, after a return journey
through Holland, Belgium, and France, he arrived
back at his studio barges on the Thames.

The tug and the barge transported inside a Rhine barge (see detail pages 36–37)

The Charts and Models

Exhibition at the Museum of Contemporary Art Antwerp (MUHKA) 1996

Rudder, Performance for a Tug, a Port, and a Museum

Quayside in front of the Museum of Contemporary Art Antwerp (MUHKA) 1996

With the University of Antwerp (RUCA), the City of Antwerp, MUHKA, Studio Herman Teirlinck acting academy, and the Port of Antwerp

The performance took place at night in November and consisted of the tugboat pulled out of the water, nine dancers and semaphorists, four television actors and one professor as speakers, and a soundtrack.

The speakers engaged in a debate in English, Dutch, German, French, and Latin. They assumed the roles of four archetypes based around the historical figures of Erasmus, Descartes, Kant, and Henry Ford. Each archetype and text represented four historical areas of influence on the present. These were ethics, philosophy, science, and business.

The dancers performed over a large area of the quayside. Their body language interpreted the texts and assisted with the communication between the different languages. The overall performance was directed by Max Couper from the wheel of his tugboat by turning the rudder, which had two powerful spotlights attached to it. Around the venue was a quadraphonic soundtrack of layered mechanical sounds constructed from the noises of the boat's machinery. On the roof of the museum was a semaphorist, who was communicating by flags with another semaphorist on the ground. Additional ambience was created by the movement of lights and sounds from ships in the port behind and a dramatic atmosphere of driving wind.

This artwork dealt with questions of communication and history combined with the idea of involving a variety of one city's institutions in a single event. It was conceived from a simple analogy: that society is steered from behind by history in the same way that a boat is steered by its rudder.

The event had grown from a collaboration between Max Couper, an artist interested in structures and mechanisms, and Emile Vanlommel, a university vice-chancellor and economist interested in art. Their joint aim was partly a perpetuation of the concept of the university as a place in which ideas can connect in universality and polarity to one another. Their collaboration, which grew into a further association with other professors and staff of the university and a free interpretation with dancers and the sound artist Ward Weis, was an organic process. It eventually led to an artwork in which the academic ideas were tempered by the unexpected broader poetry of the final event.

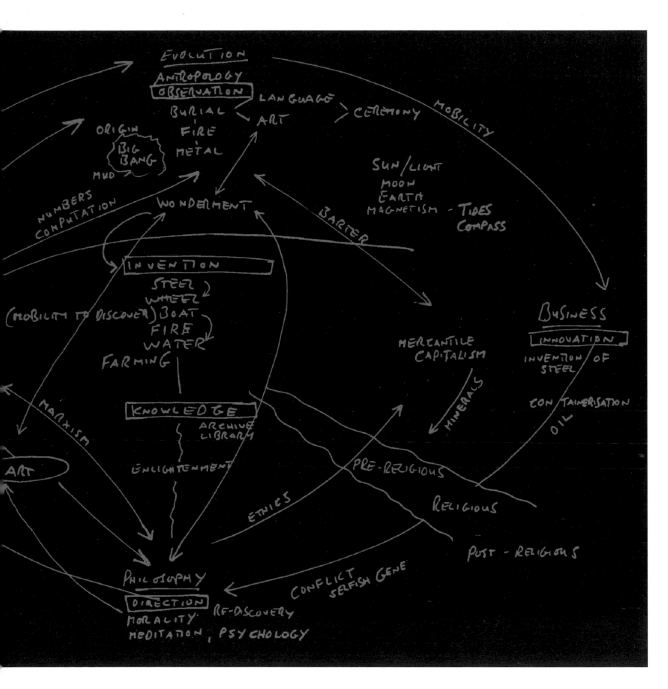

Rudder, historical flow-chart

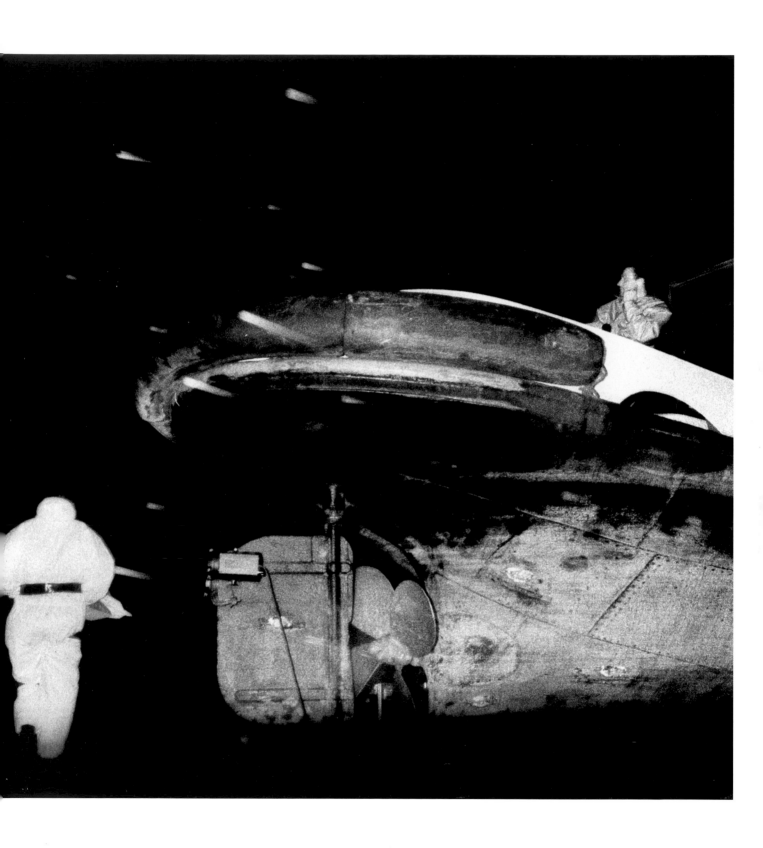

The Rhine Drawings

Ute Parduhn Gallery, by the Rhine, Kaiserswerth, Düsseldorf 1997

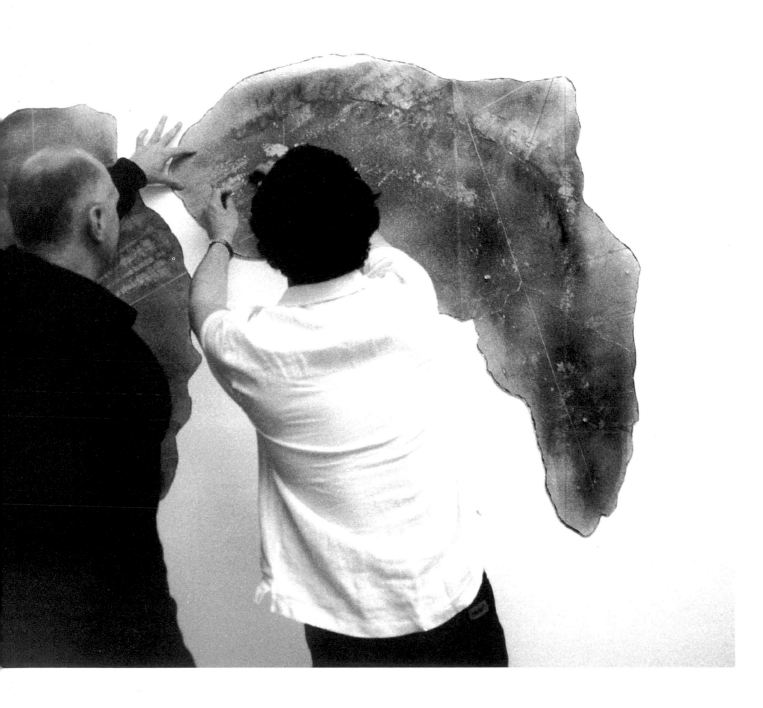

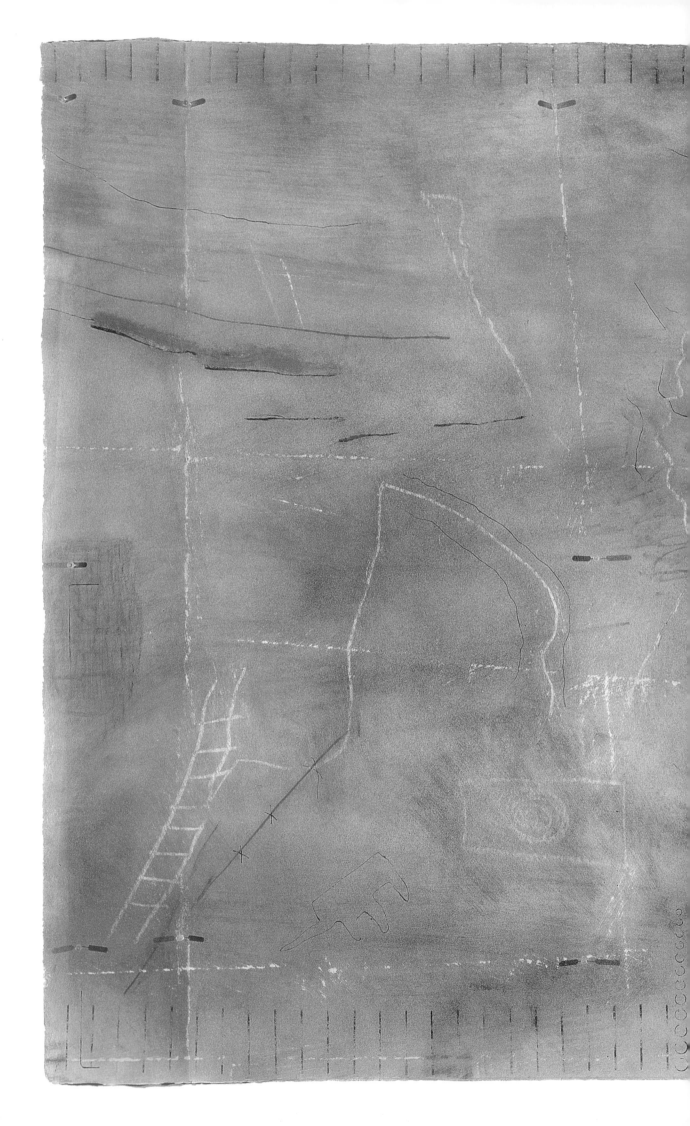

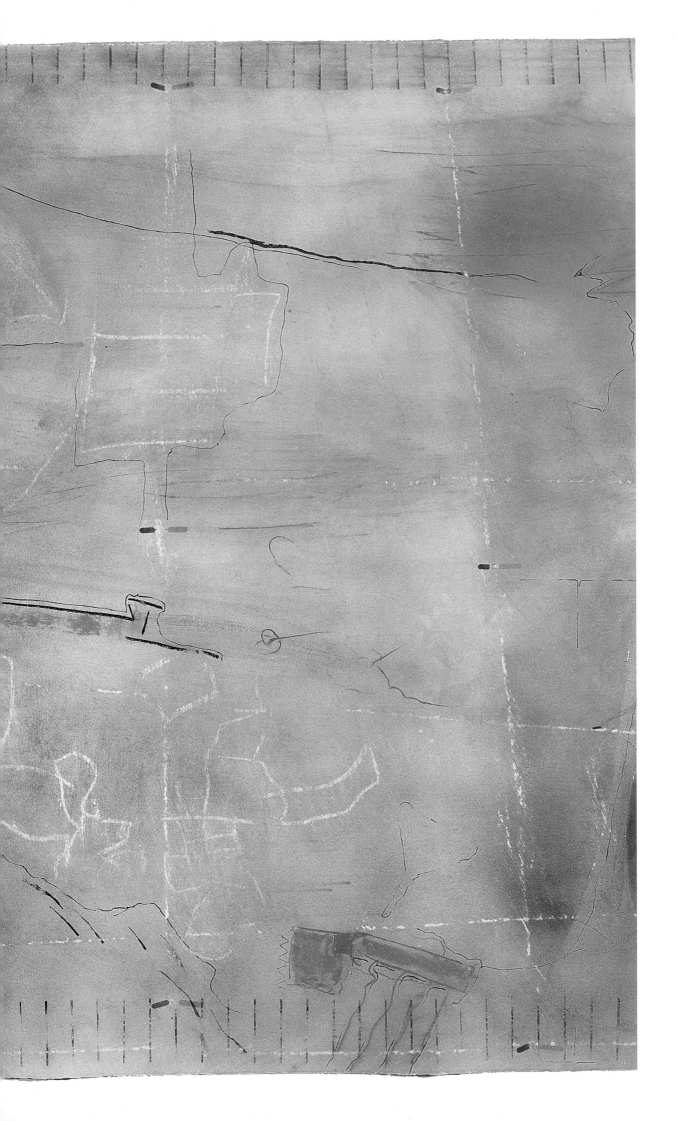

The barge inside the Rhine barge

The Eye of The Plot

Exhibition and conference

Wilhelm Lehmbruck Museum Duisburg 1997
European Centre of Modern Sculpture

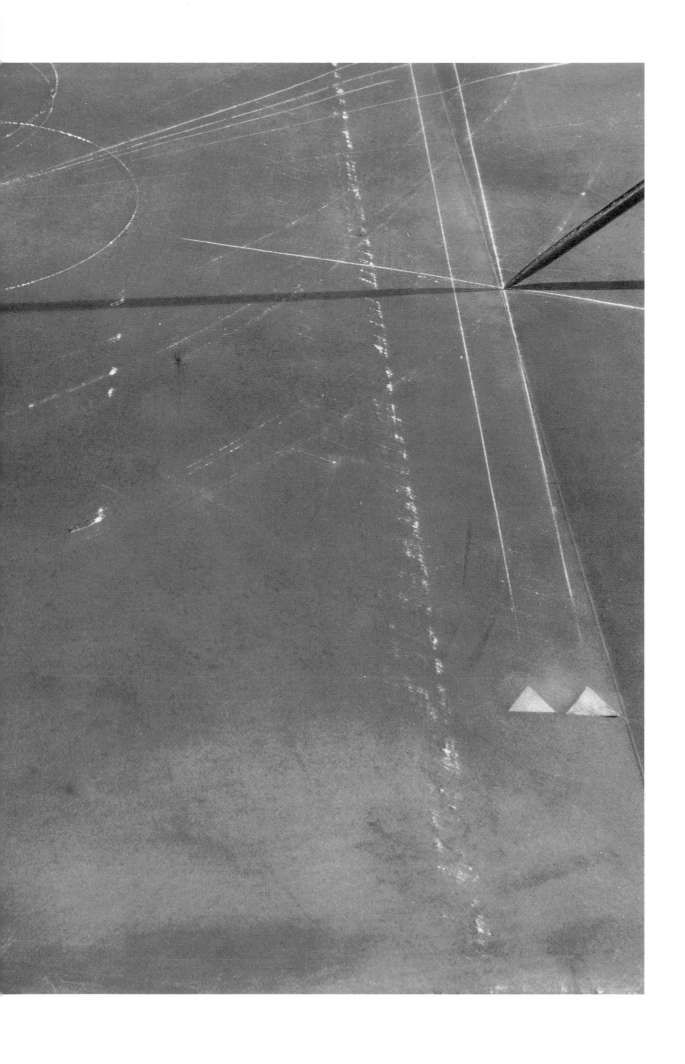

The European Business Conference Duisburg '97

Presented at the opening of *The Plot* exhibition
Part of *The Steel Fulcrum* project

Wilhelm Lehmbruck Museum Duisburg
European Centre of Modern Sculpture

Keynote speakers:

Nick Skeens (Chair)	ex British television news editor
Professor Ulrich Krempel	Director Sprengel Museum Hanover
Ute Parduhn	Ute Parduhn Gallery Düsseldorf
Terry Fox	Artist, USA
Dr Claudia Schæfer	Director Cubus Kunsthalle Duisburg
Karl Hussman	Cultural manager on behalf of Mercedes Benz
Herman Pitz	Artist, Düsseldorf
Dr Stephan von Wiese	Exhibitions director Art Museum Düsseldorf

(The following excerpt is from a transcript of the first part of the conference)

Nick Skeens
Let me raise the first issue and ask this question: What can art gain from doing business with business, and what can business gain from doing business with art? Max, how does this relate to the diagram we all have in front of us?

Max Couper
This diagram [opposite page] represents the conflicting influences on my project *The Steel Fulcrum* since I arrived in Duisburg, which have ended up being incorporated into the artwork. On the one side I am working with people from a public museum, The Lehmbruck Museum, who in turn are working to realize my projects with local partners and a corporation in the harbour. *The Steel Fulcrum*, my main project for Duisburg, started out as a metaphor for 'people and machine' but, since the problems I have encountered here in Duisburg in making it, it has become something more. More about how people, or society – a thing that we are all inside together – is balanced between the conflicting influences of business on the one side and government on the other.

In the artwork, as in society, there is a very fine balance of conflicting weights at work, which are cushioned in their effects by various checks and safeguards. The steel springs in the artwork could represent two of the main buffers protecting society. Between business and people is the buffer of public opinion – a necessary protection because otherwise business will tend towards the interests of itself and its shareholders first and foremost. The buffer between government and people is the concept of democracy and accountability. This is the much simpler relationship of the two in many ways because it is more generally understood, and it is a much older relationship than that of people and corporate big-business.

Nick Skeens
How have you tried to come to terms with this during your series of European events?

Max Couper
I have tried to give situations the chance to speak for themselves – so I don't prejudge events too much. Art is partly what happens to you. In the same way that an artist paints a picture of what he or she sees, the landscape that has confronted me here in Duisburg has been a collision of politics, business, and culture – hence what the art has become about. Since I left London and crossed the Channel last year there have been a set of different circumstances in each place. In Antwerp, for example, there was a very smooth collaboration between the city and its partners. My conclusion is one that can only come out later.

The Steel Fulcrum

(People, Government, Business)

Diagram A The Balance

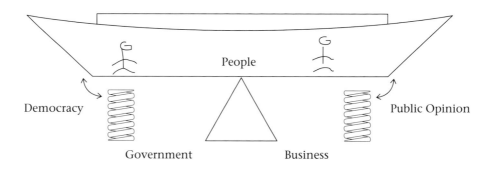

Democracy

People

Government   Business

Public Opinion

Diagram B The Relationship

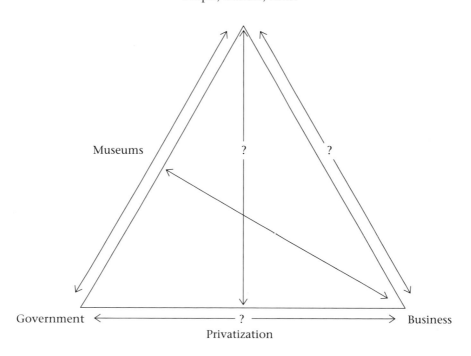

People, Culture, Artist

Museums   ?   ?

Government ←——————— ? ———————→ Business

Privatization

Nick Skeens
Let us turn to Professor Ulrich Krempel. Do you believe that as Western society develops, and many responsibilities move away from the State towards business, this is a good or a bad thing for art in general?

Professor Ulrich Krempel
I think the situation is probably very different everywhere in the world. If you look at the situation here in Germany you'll notice you still have a lot of influence and funding of culture and art by the State – which means public money – which is good for art in general. At least in democratic times this means a committed influence on the development of art. On the other side there is a natural relationship between art and business. About 490 years ago Dürer and his wife, who was a merchant, travelled to all the fairs in Europe to sell his work. At that time there were a lot of borders in what is now Europe, around which his wife worked through her commercial contacts, and they sold work. So there can be a helpful relationship between artists and people who care about the presentation and distribution of art, i.e. the dealer.

Nowadays there is a necessary relationship between all parts of society. Not far from here, in Düsseldorf, the artist Joseph Beuys, a lot of whose work is on the floor below Max Couper's exhibition here, held the view that every person working and living in different fields can be an artist in his or her specialist field – and I think there is quite a lot of truth in that. There is the possibility of intense creativity in all fields of human work. The relationship between fields can operate in a dignified or a not so dignified way. When business, as happens every day, tries to steal ideas from art, it is bad. But when there are stable and intense relations between the two it is good.

There are others who will dig deeper into this but what is obvious is that we have a complicated situation. Side A needs side B and side B needs side A, and sides A, B, and C all need each other. Without the development of ideas and a look further into the future – which is usually initiated by the artists – neither society nor business will be able to develop and we will not have real aims. And it is aims that create an intense relationship between all partners.

Nick Skeens
Taking up your term 'aims', perhaps one problem is establishing what are the aims of business in its relationship with art. I want to turn now to a representative for Mercedes Benz. Why is it that people like Mercedes Benz become involved in art projects?

Karl Hussman
As you know, Mercedes Benz do a lot of art and culture sponsoring. The aim in this is mainly to help represent the products. We see the products as the result of creativity, whose lifestyle associations can be enhanced by being linked to particular kinds of art. Also, people who enjoy culture and like art are one of the target customer groups. Sponsoring art is a means of self-representation, and in this context you could say that art serves business.

Nick Skeens
Can I have a reaction from an artist, Herman Pitz?

Herman Pitz
I am afraid, gentlemen, I can't handle this sort of approach from business.
(He walks out of the conference)

Karl Hussman
Max, as an artist you're dealing with means of transportation. I think we have something in common there.

Professor Ulrich Krempel
I am a little bit amused by this relationship that is developing between the two of you – with Max Couper who has never been in danger of being corrupted by anything. I don't think the clever art sponsorship works quite like this. I remember two kinds of art sponsorship that really looked very bad. First, when McDonalds wanted to sponsor a gallery in Hamburg and they paid for the catalogue and on the front cover you had a big McDonalds sign. That was one kind, and the second was when a big company sponsored the Munch exhibition in Essen and it was not the museum director who was the one to greet the press at the press conference but the boss of the enterprise. That is in bad taste. That doesn't work any longer.

Nick Skeens
How do you see this, Ute, as a gallerist working with Max?

Ute Parduhn
You have the gallerist in between the business and the artist, and it is our responsibility to help manage some of the problems you're seeing here today.

Max Couper
Terry, could I ask you to comment as an artist from an American perspective?

Terry Fox
I don't have any business experience. But I was involved in shows that were sponsored by business – which I didn't find out until later. In the United States it is very different. You get government funding. I think I got fifteen thousand dollars from the government five times. In the United States you get the fifteen thousand dollars but you don't have to have a specific project. You just get the money and at the end they ask you what you did with it. So you could say, well, I rented a studio and I worked but I haven't been able to have a show yet (and so on). In the United States it is very difficult to get business sponsorship.

Nick Skeens
Max, how did things work with your project for Duisburg?

Max Couper
The museum exhibition has worked well and the *Fulcrum* project for the harbour was fine. Then all kinds of bureaucracy started, creating tensions that, although I didn't realize it at first, actually enriched the tensions within the artwork, giving it an unexpected edge. Problems sometimes have a way of revealing the actual mechanisms at work below the surface. I could never have set out intentionally to create an artwork that in itself reflects all the difficulties of its own creation, which has happened with the *Fulcrum*. But in the end I may give up on making the *Fulcrum* here and make it in Düsseldorf.

Dr Claudia Schæfer
I'm sorry to hear this. With the end of public money for art it can be very difficult for artists here in Germany because business does not really understand art. Business sponsoring here is all about giving to the most famous names because there is much more publicity.

Nick Skeens
Has it not always been the case that if you were a famous name you would naturally get more support? Perhaps Dr Stephan von Wiese, curator and art historian, would comment on this?

Dr Stephan von Wiese
I would like to co-operate with more companies but they do not want to work with me because I make a programme that is not of interest to them. They want to have the big names and be sure that they promote their products. So they make exhibitions with old, famous artists who are already dead.

(Conference continues)

The European Business Conference Duisburg '97 was staged as an unannounced event, complete with conference table, in the middle of the official opening of the *The Plot* exhibition.

Couper's intention was to replicate some of the tensions that were taking place in the development for Duisburg of *The Steel Fulcrum*, the models of which were on show at the opening. The result was one of some confusion for the people attending the opening, who could not comprehend why a conference was taking place there and then, which only increased the overall irony of the event.

Despite full support from the local people, press, the city museum, and the main harbour, *The Steel Fulcrum* was eventually never made in Duisburg as intended because of difficulties at the inner-harbour corporation site. The artwork was instead transferred and realized at short notice in Düsseldorf, co-ordinated by Ute Parduhn.

Financing for the making of *The Steel Fulcrum* in Düsseldorf came from the Lehmbruck Museum, who purchased a collection of Max Couper's work for their permanent collection.

The Steel Fulcrum
(The Room that Moves when you Walk in it)

Installation for Düsseldorf harbour 1997

In association with the Art Museum, the Art Academy,
and the City of Düsseldorf

At the beginning of July, Couper's 30 ton Thames barge was hoisted out of the
water in the harbour in the centre of the city and carefully suspended at its centre
point of balance on a purpose-built steel fulcrum. Two massive springs from a
former London power station were positioned under either end.

The former cargo-hold of the barge then became a room for the public to enter.
Once inside, their combined body movement, together with a person pulling from
underneath, set the whole vessel in motion. The enormous weight of the moving
barge compressed the springs, setting off a continuous up and down pivoting
motion, which was perpetuated and controlled by the activity of the visitors.

The Steel Fulcrum was intended as an installation of human control over physical
mass, a reversal of most sculpture, where the viewer is instead a spectator of the
object's mass.

The hardest test, however, came not in making the artwork itself, which in the
end had functioned effortlessly, but in trying to overcome the mass of six months
of red tape that had prevented its realization in Duisburg – a cultural, political, and
economic process which had eventually deepened and expanded the original idea
of the artwork.

The final artwork can be seen as a simple metaphor, of society as a room that we
are all in together; a society built – as is the work of art itself – on the remnants of
an industrial past and whose equilibrium and future direction is determined by the
way in which we decide to walk together.

Tug Print
A Contemporary Archaeology

Installation for the Sprengel Museum
of modern art Hanover 1997

At the end of July, Max Couper's tugboat was lifted out by
harbour crane at Hanover's Lindener Harbour and
transported by road into the museum, where it was
dropped from five metres into a mound of 100 tons of
Hanover clay and sand. It was then removed to leave
behind the imprint of its underbelly: the *Tug Print*.

    The tug then returned to London, whilst the *Tug Print*
remained in situ, slowly cracking up until it was finally
obliterated by the weather.

    This was an artwork that had developed in three quite
separate ways. First an original accidental imprint had
been made some years earlier in a muddy creek of the east
coast of England. Then there was the spectacle and
performance of making the print in the museum,
broadcast on international television. And finally there
was the aftermath, in which the print had become a silent
part of the museum's collection – begging the question of
the visitor of what had made it – obvious only that it must
have come from above.

    The final installation, devoid of the boat, has resonances
of archaic ceremony and monument-making of burial or
fertility – centred on the imprint of a petroleum-powered
machine. It is a deliberate distortion, a way of looking at
the present as though it was already a trace from the
distant past.

The tug pushing the barge down the River Schel

Front and back cover
Three Balls on a Museum
Installation outside The Plot exhibition, Museum of Contemporary Art, Antwerp, 1996
3 steel anchor balls suspended in a line, hung from the roof onto the
front wall of the museum, with the tug in the distance on the quayside
Each ball 41cm (16in) diameter
Photograph: Edward Woodman

Inside front cover flap
The Plot exhibition, Museum of Contemporary Art, Antwerp, 1996
View from the telescope of The Chart Room installation in the museum,
fixed on the tug and the location of The Rudder performance on the quayside
of the River Schelde behind
Photograph: Edward Woodman

Pages 2–3
Anatomy of a Flying Tug
View of the underbelly of Couper's tug Pablo
Thames tosher tug: 1070 × 305cm (35 × 10ft)
Photograph: Max Couper

Page 6–7
Proximity Chart (detail)
Mixed-media assemblage of maps and glass, 1995
Shows the general location of The Plot series
53 × 64 × 3cm (21 × 25 × 1in)
Photograph: Edward Woodman

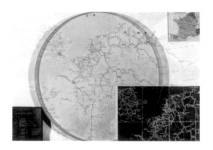

Pages 10–11
Crossing the Channel
10km northwest of Calais in the shipping lanes
Couper's tug Pablo with the Thames barge in tow
behind with the Blue Board rotating priority signal
in the foreground; Luise Seppeler at the helm
Photograph: Max Couper

Pages 12–13
*Up the Rhine, Inside an Ore Barge, In the Fog with Radar, In Front of a
Rhine Push Tug, With 3000 Tons of Acid Alongside in Another Barge*
Couper's tug and barge (centre top) loaded in a Rhine barge for
transportation from Rotterdam to Duisburg, 1996
Part of the Lembruck Museum Steel Fulcrum project
Photograph: Max Couper

Pages 14–15
The Chart Room installation
View of part of the installation, looking through to The Model Room
The Plot exhibition, Museum of Contemporary Art, Antwerp, 1996
Charts of pigment, spray paint, acrylic, chalk, and pen, on watercolour paper,
enclosed in glass chart-cases
Sand Bars Chart (to right): 160 × 453 × 10cm (5ft 3in × 14ft 10fiin × 4in)
Photograph: Edward Woodman

Pages 16–17
The Model Room installation
Second room of The Plot exhibition, Museum of Contemporary Art, Antwerp, 1996
Right to left on floor: Tug Print remote-controlled model;
The Hold mechanical model; The Rudder radio-controlled model
With proposal sketches from The Plot series on the walls behind
Photograph: Edward Woodman

Pages 18–19
The Chart Room installation
The Plot exhibition, Museum of Contemporary Art, Antwerp, 1996
View of The Plotting Table: steel table with variable plotting instrument and
two stellar charts of pigment, spray paint, graphite, and chalk, on watercolour paper
206 × 460 × 236cm (6ft 9in × 15ft 3in × 7ft 9in)
Photograph: Edward Woodman

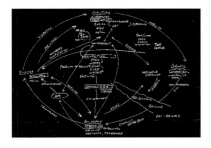

Pages 20–21
The Historical Rudder
University of Antwerp (RUCA), 1996
Thematic flow chart and simplification model
Pen on paper, reversed
From a seminar by Max Couper with students of Professor Vanlommel,
project collaborator, during residence at the university whilst collaborating
on the texts of the Rudder performance

Pages 22–27
Rudder, Performance for a Tug, a Port, and a Museum
Quayside, Museum of Contemporary Art, Antwerp, 1996
In collaboration with Professor Dr Emile Vanlommel
Actors: Karen Vanparijs, Ludo Busschots, Caroline Van Gastel,
          Nick Skeens, Professor Emeritus Clem Neutjens
Movement and Dance: Sanderijn Helsen, Kristien De Proost, Stijn Cole,
          Stijn Van Ostal, Eva Schram, Nele Goosens and Geert Rampelberg of
          Studio Herman Teirlinck; Daniel Vidovsky; Carlos De Haro
Coordination: Veerle Emboo
Research: Glenn Rayp; Professor Verluyten and Theo Joos of RUCA;
          Michael Oukhow
Choreography: Toon Van Ishoven
Sound: Ward Weis
Photographs: Michael Wiegandt

Pages 28–29
Tectonic Chart
Exhibition of charts, Ute Parduhn Gallery, Kaiserswerth, Düsseldorf, 1997
Pigment, spray paint, acrylic, and pen, on watercolour paper
During hanging of the first two of several sections of the chart,
Max Couper to the right

Pages 30–31
Land Chart
Detail of left half of chart
Exhibition of charts, Ute Parduhn Gallery, Düsseldorf, 1997
Pigment, spray paint, acrylic, pastel, candle wax, and pen, on watercolour paper
152 × 380cm (5ft × 12ft 5in) overall
Photograph: Edward Woodman

Pages 32–33
Stellar Chart, Scale One to Infinity
Installation view
Exhibition of charts, Ute Parduhn Gallery, Düsseldorf, 1997
Photograph: Max Couper

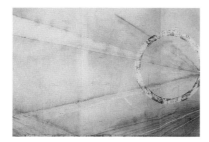

Pages 34–35
Stellar Chart, Scale One to Infinity
Spray paint, acrylic, pencil, and chalk, on watercolour paper
152 × 450cm (5ft × 14ft 9in)
Photograph: Edward Woodman

Pages 36–37
Barge in Barge
Couper's Thames barge from London inside a Rhine ore barge
during transportation up the Rhine to Duisburg
Part of the Lehmbruck Museum Steel Fulcrum project
Photograph: Max Couper

Pages 38–39
The Plot exhibition
Lehmbruck Museum, Duisburg, 1997
Installation view with topographical floor chart of pigment, spray paint, acrylic, chalk, and pen, on watercolour paper (foreground)
152 × 450cm (5ft × 14ft 10in) when unfolded
Tug Print model and The Steel Fulcrum base elements (background)
Photograph: Max Couper

Pages 40–41
Stellar Chart (earth curvature version)
Detail of left half of chart
Pigment, spray paint, graphite, and chalk, on watercolour paper with plotting instrument
Photograph: Edward Woodman

Page 42–43
The Plot exhibition
Lehmbruck Museum, Duisburg, 1997
Steel fulcrum substructure and springs of The Steel Fulcrum (foreground);
charts and models (background)
Photograph: Max Couper

Pages 44–47
The European Business Conference, Duisburg '97
Presented at the opening of The Plot exhibition,
Lehmbruck Museum, Duisburg, 1997
Part of The Steel Fulcrum project
Keynote speakers, left to right: Karl Hussman; Ute Parduhn; Nick Skeens;
Professor Ulrich Krempel; Dr Claudia Schaefer; Max Couper;
Claudia Grundei; Dr Stephen von Wiese; Marita Looser; Terry Fox

Pages 44–47
The European Business Conference, Duisburg '97
Lehmbruck Museum, Duisburg, 1997
The London delegation, on route from London
Left to right: Max Couper; Nick Skeens; Peter Wilder

Pages 48–49
The Steel Fulcrum
The steel fulcrum substructure of the installation
Düsseldorf Harbour, 1997
Steel fulcrum (heavy version) in two sections
Overall 72 × 82 × 400cm (28in × 32in × 13ft 1in)
Photograph: Edward Woodman

Pages 50–51
The Steel Fulcrum
Harbour stevedores setting out the base elements before balancing
the barge in position on top
Düsseldorf Harbour, 1997
Photograph: Luise Seppeler

Pages 52–53
The Steel Fulcrum
Installation, Düsseldorf Harbour, 1997
Couper's 30 ton 1930s Thames barge, balanced and pivoting on a
steel fulcrum with springs under either end, set in motion by the movement
of the public participants inside and perpetuated by the action of the springs.
Photograph shows Max Couper increasing motion by rope and Professor Fritz Swegler
of the Düsseldorf Art Academy on the barge with television tower to his left.
Overall dimension of installation: 275 × 430 × 1830cm (9ft × 14ft × 60ft)
Photograph: Bernd Nanninga

Pages 54–55
Force and Reaction
View of the load-bearing steel fulcrum and one of the two reciprocating steel springs
under the barge. (The springs originate from a set that once supported the vibrating main
turbine of the now defunct Fulham power station in west London.)
Düsseldorf Harbour, 1997
Each spring: 64 × 34cm (25in × 13in)
Photograph: Max Couper

Pages 56–57
The Fulcrum and Bundles of Steel
View of the installation of The Steel Fulcrum
(with the overhead crane that lifted the barge into position in the background)
Düsseldorf Harbour, 1997
Photograph: Max Couper

Pages 58–59
Tug Print
Couper's tug being hoisted out of the water in Lindener Harbour, Hanover,
before being transported by low-loader through the city to the Sprengel Museum
for the making of the Tug Print installation, 1997
Photograph shows Max Couper positioning the boat out of the water by rope
Photograph: Michael Herling

Pages 60–61
Tug Print
The tug in the Sprengel Museum just before being dropped from 5 metres into a
mound of 100 tons of Hanover clay and sand
Photograph taken during the public performance of the making of the Tug Print
installation
Sprengel Museum, Hanover, 1997
Photograph: Michael Herling

Pages 62–63
Tug Print
The 20 ton tug implanting the impression of its hull in the clay
and sand of the installation just after being dropped
Sprengel Museum, Hanover, 1997
Photograph: Michael Herling

Pages 64–65
Tug Print the installation
Impression of the tugboat's hull in clay and sand
Sprengel Museum, Hanover, 1997
View of the installation drying out and starting to crack
after the making of the impression
150 × 1500 × 500cm (5ft × 50ft × 14ft) approx.
Photograph: Michael Herling

Pages 66–67
Tug Print the installation
Sprengel Museum, Hanover, 1997
Aerial view from the roof of the museum
Photograph: Max Couper

Pages 68–69
Tug Print the installation
Sprengel Museum, Hanover, 1997
Panoramic view of the Tug Print and the museum
Photograph: Max Couper

Pages 70–71
Down the Schelde
Couper's tug pushing the barge with the tide down the River Schelde
from Gent to Antwerp, Belgium
Flor Bex at the helm
Photograph: Max Couper

Pages 78–79
Origin of The Plot
Imprint of the tug's underbelly in mud at low tide
Faversham, Kent, 1994
Photograph: Max Couper

Inside back cover flap
Couper's tug *Pablo*
Built Wivenhoe, Essex, 1952, fitted with a 180 h.p. Gardner 6-cylinder diesel engine
305 × 1070cm (10ft × 35ft). Draught 150cm (5ft)
Photographed on the quayside in front of the Museum of Contemporary Art,
Antwerp, 1996, in position for the Rudder performance, part of The Plot exhibition
Photograph: Edward Woodman

The exhibitions and events of *The Plot* series were organized on location by:

Flor Bex   Director of the Museum of Contemporary Art Antwerp
Ernest Van Buynder   President of the Museum of Contemporary Art Antwerp
Professor Emile Vanlommel   Vice Chancellor of Antwerp University (RUCA)
Dr Christoph Brockhaus   Director of the Lehmbruck Museum Duisburg
Ute Parduhn   The Ute Parduhn Gallery Düsseldorf
Professor Ulrich Krempel   Director of the Sprengel Museum Hanover

General assistance and boat crew for *The Plot* series:

Luise Seppeler (co-navigator)
Edward Woodman
Peter Wilder
Nick Skeens
Flor Bex
Veerle Emboo
Elizabeth Weymann
Karl Geist
Sabina Beckman

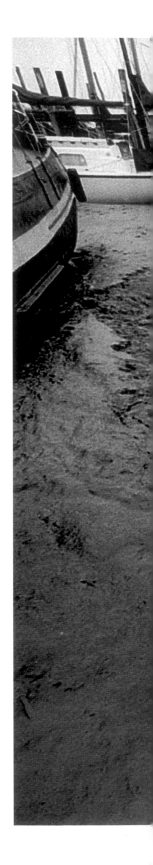

Tug Print, Faversham, Kent, England 1994